The Church

by
Donald Dean Smeeton

---

*Developed in Cooperation With
the ICI International Office Staff*

*Instructional Development Specialist:
A. Juanita Cunningham*

Illustrator: Carmen Kinney

International Correspondence Institute
6300 N. Belt Line Road
Irving, TX 75063
USA

Address of the ICI office in your area:

Scripture quotations are from the New International Version (NIV) and Good News Bible (Today's English Version). © American Bible Society, 1976. Used by permission. The King James Version (KJV) is also quoted.

First Edition 1978
Second Edition 1980
Third Edition 1982
Fourth Edition 1984
Fifth Edition 1986
Sixth Edition 1991
    Reprint 1992   6/92 3M BA

© 1978, 1980, 1982, 1984, 1986, 1991
All Rights Reserved
International Correspondence Institute

ISBN 1-56390-007-6

contents

page

First, Let's Have a Talk 5

Lesson

1 God's Plan for the Church 10

2 The History of the Church 22

3 What the Church Is 38

4 How I Can Be a Part of God's Church 50

5 How the Church is Like a Body 64

6 What the Church Does for Itself 76

7 What the Church Does for the World 86

8 What the Church Does for God 98

first, let's have a talk

From Your Study Guide Author

Have you ever wondered where the church came from, how it got started, what will happen to it in the future? If you have read the titles of the lessons in this book, you will see that they answer important questions about the church.

I want to help you study the answers to these questions. You have not met me, but I want to be your friend as well as your teacher. As we study together what the Bible says about the church, we will get a better understanding of our place in the church. There are many different ideas about the church. Some of these ideas are true, but others are false. We will see what the Bible says about them.

This course does not only tell you about the church, but it will also help you to know how you can be more useful to Christ and His church, as you put into practice what you learn. The modern method of teaching yourself helps you to learn the principles easily and begin practicing them immediately. Let the Holy Spirit speak to you as you study.

About the Author

By the time your author, Donald Dean Smeeton, was ordained by the Assemblies of God in 1973, he had already pioneered a Pentecostal fellowship group among the military in Germany and started the Teen Challenge program in Belgium. In 1973 he began teaching at Continental Bible College in Brussels, Belgium, and continued there for nine years. In 1982 he joined the staff of ICI in Brussels.

Academically he is well prepared to write about the church of Jesus Christ. He obtained a B.S. and a B.A. before completing an M.A. cum laude in Church History and the History of Christian Thought from Trinity Evangelical Divinity School, Deerfield, Illinois. He then studied at the *Faculté de Théologie Protestante* at the University of Strasbourg, France, and more recently completed a Ph.D. from the University of Louvain in Belgium. He is a frequent contributor to academic journals.

Your Study Guide

The Church is a pocket-sized workbook that you can take with you and study whenever you have some free time. Try to set aside some time every day to study it.

Be sure to study carefully the first two pages of each lesson. This prepares your mind for what follows. Next, study the lesson, section by section, and follow the instructions under the title, *For You to Do*. If there is not room to write your answers in the study guide, write them in a notebook so you can refer to them when you review the lesson.

If you are studying this course with a group, follow the instructions of your group leader.

How to Answer Study Questions

There are different kinds of study questions in this study guide. Following are samples of several types and how to answer them.

A *MULTIPLE-CHOICE* question or item asks you to choose an answer from the ones that are given.

Example of Multiple-Choice Question

1 A week has a total of
a) 10 days.
b) 7 days.
c) 5 days.

The correct answer is *b) 7 days*. In your study guide, make a circle around *b)* as shown here:

1 A week has a total of
a) 10 days.
(b)) 7 days.
c) 5 days.

(For some multiple-choice items, more than one answer may be correct. In that case, you would circle the letter in front of each correct answer.)

A *TRUE-FALSE* question or item asks you to choose which of several statements are TRUE.

Example of a True-False Question

2 Which statements below are TRUE?
a   The Bible has a total of 120 books.
ⓑ   The Bible is a message for believers today.
c   All of the Bible authors wrote in the Hebrew language
ⓓ   The Holy Spirit inspired the writers of the Bible.

Statements **b** and **d** are true. You would make a circle around these two letters to show your choices, as you see above.

A *MATCHING* question or item asks you to match things that go together, such as names with descriptions, or Bible books with their authors.

Example of Matching Question

3 Write the number for the leader's name in front of each phrase that describes something he did.

..**1**.**a** Received the Law at Mt. Sinai   1) Moses
..**2**.**b** Led the Israelites across Jordan   2) Joshua
..**2**.**c** Marched around Jericho
..**1**.**d** Lived in Pharaoh's court

Phrases **a** and **d** refer to *Moses,* and phrases **b** and **c** refer to *Joshua*. You would write **1** beside **a** and **d**, and **2** beside **b** and **c**, as you see above.

Your Student Report

If you are studying to earn a certificate or a seal, you have received a separate booklet called *Student Report Question Booklet: The Church.* There are two sections in this booklet with a separate answer sheet for each one. Your study guide will tell you when to complete each section.

Follow the instructions given in your student report for sending the answer sheets to the ICI office in your area. The address should be stamped in the front of this study guide or on the back of the student report

First, Let's Have a Talk

question booklet. If it is not there, send the answer sheets to the ICI Brussels address given on the back of the student report question booklet. When you do this, you will receive an attractive certificate. Or if you have already earned the certificate by completing another course in this unit of courses, you will receive a seal.

Objectives

You will notice that *objectives* are given at the beginning of each lesson. The word *objective* is used in this book to help you know what to expect from your study. An *objective* is like a goal, or a purpose. You will study better if you keep in mind your *objectives*.

Now you are ready to begin Lesson 1. God bless you as you study!

lesson 1: God's plan for the church

Jesus said, "I will build my church, and not even death will ever be able to overcome it" (Matthew 16:18). This is a wonderful promise! This verse tells us several important things about the church. Let us list them:

1. The church is Jesus' church—"My church."
2. Jesus has a plan for His church—"I will build."
3. Jesus' church will not be defeated—"Not even death will ever be able to overcome it."

God had a plan for the church from the beginning of the world. It was a hidden plan. Then, at the right time, God revealed His plan. We will see that God's plan reaches into the future also. God has prepared great things for us! Even if we have problems now, we can look in faith to the future.

In this lesson you will study...

The Beginning of the Church
The Glorious Future of the Church
Present Condition of the Church
    The Purpose of the Church
    The Suffering of the Church

This lesson will help you...

- Explain when God's plan for the church really started.
- Identify Jesus' role in God's plan for the church.
- Relate God's eternal plan to present problems.

THE BEGINNING OF THE CHURCH

Objective 1. *Tell how God's plan for the church began.*

Where did the church come from? Perhaps the church has been in your area for many centuries, or for only a short time. Perhaps someone in your community began preaching the gospel, or maybe someone came from another place to tell about Christ.

Before the gospel came to your area—even before *anyone* knew the gospel—God had a plan. God's plan did not begin in your lifetime. It did not begin at the cross where Jesus died. God's plan began before He created the world. Paul told the church at Ephesus about this plan:

> Even before the world was made, God had already chosen us to be his through our union with Christ, so that we would be holy and without fault before him. Because of his love God had already decided that through Jesus Christ he would make us his sons—this was his pleasure and purpose (Ephesians 1:4-5).

God's Plan for the Church

Then, at the right time, Jesus came. (See Galatians 4:4.) Jesus taught the truth about God and did many miracles. Men refused to accept Him. They crucified Him. But God raised Jesus back to life!

Jesus began his ministry among the Jews. Many of the Jews refused Jesus. But God went right on working out His plan. Again Paul explained this to the church at Ephesus:

> In past times mankind was not told this secret, but God has revealed it now by the Spirit to his holy apostles and prophets. The secret is that by means of the gospel the Gentiles have a part with the Jews in God's blessing; they are members of the same body and share in the promise that God made through Jesus Christ (Ephesians 3:5-6).

The church, then, is all those who believe in Christ, from every nation. Through the gospel, they have now become part of His church.

For You to Do

In each one of these *For You to Do* sections, the questions or exercises will help you review or apply what you have studied.

1 Circle the letter of the statement which is true:
  a God's plan began when Jesus died.
  b God's plan began with the creation of people.
  c God was working out His plan for the church from the beginning.

2 Read again Ephesians 3:5-6. Write in your own words the answers to the following questions:

a How did God reveal His plan?

....

....

b What was God's plan?

....

....

Check your answers with the answers given at the end of this lesson.

THE GLORIOUS FUTURE OF THE CHURCH

Objective 2. *State how God's plan for the future of the church involves Christ.*

God was working out His plan through Christ. Man's rejection of Christ did not stop God. Christ's death did not stop Him. God kept on working out His plan.

God has a plan for the future, too! At the right time, God will finish His plan. He has not been defeated. He *will not* be defeated! The Bible tells us some of the things God has in store for His church. Just before Jesus was put to death, He prayed:

Father! You have given them to me, and I want them to be with me where I am, so that they may

God's Plan for the Church

see my glory, the glory you gave me; for you loved me before the world was made (John 17:24).

Sometime—at the right time—God will answer that prayer. Some day the church will be with Jesus and we will see His glory. No one knows completely what heaven will be like, but it will be wonderful to be with Jesus Christ!

The Bible tells us how this will happen. Jesus will come to earth again for His church. Paul told the church at Thessalonica about this event:

There will be the shout of command, the archangel's voice, the sound of God's trumpet, and the Lord himself will come down from heaven. Those who have died believing in Christ will rise to life first; then we who are living at that time will be gathered up along with them in the clouds to meet the Lord in the air. And so we will always be with the Lord (1 Thessalonians 4:16-17).

We do not know when this will happen. It could be very soon. God knows the right time.

For You to Do

3 In the following sentences, write in the correct word or words.

   a Because God has fulfilled his plan in the past, we can have faith in Him for the ....

   b One of the most glorious things about heaven is that we will be with ....

   c When Jesus comes for His church, there will be the sound of ....
....

   d Believers, both living and dead, will meet together with the ....

4 In John 17:24 Jesus asked in His prayer that
a) God would love us more.
b) we would be with Him in heaven.
c) the Father would give the church to Him.

5 Read Revelation 22:3-5. Who will rule with Christ in heaven?
a) The angels
b) The prophets and apostles
c) All servants of God

6 Explain now, what God's future plan is for His church.

....

Check your answers.

PRESENT CONDITION OF THE CHURCH

The church has a wonderful past and a glorious future, but it must live on earth now. We do not live in eternity, past or future, but we live *now*. How can these truths we have studied help us now?

The Purpose of the Church

Objective 3. *List two of the present purposes of the church.*

Later we will look at the duties of the church in more detail, but now we must see some overall goals. We read in Paul's letter to the church at Ephesus:

> God gave me this privilege ... of making all people see how God's secret plan is to be put into effect. God, who is the Creator of all things, kept his secret hidden through all the past ages, in order that at the present time, by means of the church, the angelic rulers and powers in the heavenly world might learn of his wisdom in all its different forms (Ephesians 3:8-10).

The words *heavenly world* mean "the area of spiritual conflict." The words *angelic rulers and powers* mean "the evil spirits which cause men to do evil." Paul explains that God's purpose for the church is to defeat the evil spirits in this world.

Look at the rest of chapter 3. The Bible says that because the church's purpose is to defeat evil, we can come boldly before God in prayer (Ephesians 3:11-13).

Also because of this, we stand strong in God's power (Ephesians 3:14-16). Finally, we must be united in love (Ephesians 3:17-19).

A second general purpose of the church is found in the last few verses of this chapter.

> To him [God] who by means of this power working in us is able to do so much more than we can ever ask for, or even think of: to God be the glory in the church and in Christ Jesus for all time, for ever and ever! Amen (Ephesians 3:20-21).

For You to Do

7 Look at Ephesians 3 again. State in your own words two purposes for the church:

   a verses 8-10 ....
   ....

   b verses 20-21 ....
   ....

Check your answers.

The Suffering of the Church

Objective 4. *Explain why Christians sometimes suffer.*

Sometimes Christians suffer because of their belief in Christ. Sometimes the church is harmed. Maybe you have been treated badly because you are a Christian. Sometimes people are hurt or misunderstood and other people fight against them because of what they believe. This is called *persecution*.

Such pain is hard to understand. Sometimes you might ask, "If God has such great things planned for me, why am I hurting now?" This question is not easy. Let us look at what the Bible says.

1. *Some suffering is normal.* Everyone goes through times of suffering, whether one is a Christian or not. Even Christians must suffer. Paul told the young man, Timothy: "Everyone who wants to live a godly life in Christ Jesus will be persecuted" (2 Timothy 3:12). But it is wonderful to know that when we suffer God is with us and He gives us strength.

2. *Suffering is a privilege.* We know that it is an honor to suffer for Christ. Because God has special rewards for those who are persecuted, it is special. Paul told the church at Philippi, "For you have been given the privilege of serving Christ not only by believing in him, but also by suffering for him" (Philippians 1:29).

3. *Suffering is temporary.* Suffering will not last. Paul wrote to the church at Rome, "I consider that what we suffer at this present time cannot be compared at all with the glory that is going to be revealed to us" (Romans 8:18).

4. *Suffering is rewarded.* During periods of suffering, we can look to the future. We look beyond earth to heaven. God will reward us. The Bible says, "If we continue to endure, we shall also rule with him" (2 Timothy 2:12). God is keeping a record. As we have seen, God has great things planned for the church. We

can be a part of that great future. But we must be faithful now even during difficulty.

You might say, "My father has rejected me because I am a Christian." That is painful. But such suffering is normal. You can say, "God has rewarded me with many spiritual fathers. This pain, and many others, I will leave behind when Jesus comes for his church."

For You to Do

8 In view of God's eternal plan, why is the church sometimes persecuted?

....
....
....

Check your answers.

Congratulations! You have finished the first lesson. We have moved from the beginning of time to eternity in heaven in 11 pages. We have seen the church's beginning and its end. In the next lesson we will try to arrive at a biblical definition of the church. What did Jesus mean when he said, "I will build my church?"

Check Your Answers

The answers to your study exercises are not given in the usual order, so that you will not see the answer to your next question ahead of time. Look for the number you need, and try not to look ahead.

8 Your answer should include these points: Suffering is normal for everyone. It is an honor to suffer for Christ. We are willing to suffer now, because we will be rewarded later.

1 c) God was working out His plan for the church from the beginning.

7 a To defeat evil.
  b To bring glory to God.
  (Your answer should have the same meaning.)

2 a By the Holy Spirit through the apostles and prophets.
  b That both Jews and Gentiles would enjoy God's blessings through Jesus Christ.

6 Jesus Christ will come again for His church (His people). For eternity, the church will be with Him and rule with Him.

3 a future.
  b the Lord Jesus Christ.
  c (any of these) the shout of command, the archangel's voice, the trumpet of God.
  d Lord.

5 c) All servants of God.

4 b) we would be with Him in heaven.

lesson 2: the history of the church

In the first lesson, we saw the church from the viewpoint of eternity. God planned the church. At the right time God revealed His plan. In spite of problems we might have now, God is working in His church. One day, God will finish His plans for the church. Jesus will come to earth again and He will take the church to be with Him in heaven.

Now, we will look at the church from the viewpoint of the earth. When Jesus said, "I will build my church," He implied "here on the earth." In this lesson we will take a very brief look at what happened from Pentecost to the present.

We can learn much from history. It is exciting to see how the church grew. But, as we will see, there were problems along the way, and these problems teach us many lessons. I find church history very interesting. I'm sure you will, too.

In This Lesson You Will Study ...

The Church Is Born
The Church Is Made Legal
The Church Is Damaged
The Church Is Reformed
The Church Is Revived

This Lesson Will Help You ...

- Trace the history of the church.
- Understand the cause of some of the problems in the church.
- Define a number of organizational patterns in the church.

THE CHURCH IS BORN

Objective 1. *Describe what happened on the Day of Pentecost and the events that followed.*

Pentecost was a great Jewish holiday. It was at harvest time. Many people came great distances to be in Jerusalem. On the first Pentecost after Jesus rose from the dead, his followers gathered in Jerusalem. Something special happened! Rather than my telling you, you can find out what happened by doing the following:

For You to Do

1 Read Acts 2:1-5, looking for the answers to the following questions:

  a When did this take place? ....

  b What two strange things happened in the room? ....

  c What happened to the disciples?

  ....

2 What was the reaction of the crowd (Acts 2:13)?

....

The History of the Church

3 How did Peter explain to the crowd on the Day of Pentecost who the Messiah was (Acts 2:36)?

....

4 Place a circle around the letters in front of the statements below that tell what the early believers did (Acts 2:42).
   a They learned from the apostles.
   b They prayed together.
   c They had fellowship.
   d They argued with each other.
   e They ate together.

Check your answers.

The church had a wonderful beginning. There were many new converts (Acts 2:41) and the church grew daily (v. 47). But very soon trouble started. God's enemies fought His church. The book of Acts records some of the suffering (4:23; 5:17-18).

People told lies about the believers. Some heard part of the message, but changed it into something false. The Roman government did not like the Christian groups. Christians were accused of being bad citizens. Many early Christians suffered. Some were tortured, and many were killed. But truth cannot be killed.

The believers were forced to leave their homes; they went to Parthia, Mesopotamia, Egypt, Libya, and even to the capital city, Rome. Everywhere they went, Christians told of what God had done. New groups of believers were started in many places.

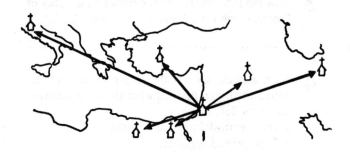

For You to Do

5 Look at the map. The arrows show how the early Christians spread to other areas. In spite of the trouble, what happened to the church?

....

THE CHURCH IS MADE LEGAL

Objective 2. *State why the church began to organize itself.*

Much of the book of Acts tells us how the message spread. It describes the work of Paul and Peter. Many of the books of the New Testament are letters which Paul wrote to the new churches. Finally, there were so many Christians in the Roman Empire that even some of the emperors became Christians! Emperor Constantine (about 300 years after the birth of Christ) made Christianity legal. Many people joined the church because everyone else was joining. Some did not even know God. They joined the church as people would join a club, without really becoming Christians. Of course this caused some confusion, because the true *church* is made up of those who accept Christ.

In spite of confusion, there was at all times a true church, made up of faithful Christians. And it grew rapidly.

With this growth came the need to organize the church so the people could work well together. The widows needed help, so deacons were chosen (Acts 6:1-4). The church had other needs too. It needed to be protected from evil men, and from men who did not teach the truth. The bigger churches needed to help the smaller ones. They needed to be better organized so they could work together in unity.

For You to Do

6 Circle the letter in front of the answer which best completes this sentence. The church needed to be organized
   a) because the emperor became a Christian.
   b) so it could better provide help, protection, and unity.
   c) to make it legal.

THE CHURCH IS DAMAGED

Objective 3. *Explain why problems developed in the church.*

As time went on, the Christian emperors (rulers) tried to control the church, and the church became involved in politics. Church leaders, called *bishops,* fought to have power in the big cities. Some people in the church had forgotten its purpose for being.

About 500 years after the birth of Christ, Rome itself was destroyed. By A.D. 1000, Christians in the East had nothing to do with Christians in the West.

Because they wanted to get away from sin, which was found both inside and outside of the church, some Christians withdrew. They separated themselves from the world and from less spiritual Christians. They entered special communities called *monasteries*. Monasteries usually had high walls around them to keep the world outside.

Is it good for Christians to live in a monastery? This question is hard to answer. There were some good things that came from monasteries, and some bad. Sometimes monasteries were centers of learning. Sometimes the people from them were the first to take the Christian teaching to a new area. They helped to bring the gospel to Europe about A.D. 500, to England about A.D. 700, and to Scandinavia about A.D. 1000.

The History of the Church   29

But there were also problems. The monastery walls separated those inside from other people and their needs. They could not help the world this way. Sometimes the men and women inside were more concerned about their own souls than those of others. Often monasteries became places of sin. The walls could not keep out sin.

For You to Do

7 Circle the reason that best explains why the church began to have problems.
  a) It got too big.
  b) People quit going to church.
  c) The church forgot that it was supposed to minister to peoples' needs.
  d) The Christians wanted to be with sinful people.

THE CHURCH IS REFORMED

Objective 4. *List three biblical teachings restored by Luther.*

As the years went by, many errors came into the church. Pagan (ungodly) ceremonies replaced the freedom of the Holy Spirit. Pagan religions were changed a little so they appeared to be Christian. Membership in the church organization became more important than a godly life. Baptized people were considered Christians even if they continued to live like pagans. When men tried to call the church back to biblical truth, they were rejected. When God sent revival, the leaders were often put to death.

Changes in Teaching

But in the early 1500s, a spiritual change began. It started with a man in a monastery. His name was Martin Luther. He had tried to find God. He obeyed the church. He hid from the world. He starved himself and beat his body. But he could not find God. After several years, he started to study the Bible. There he found his answer. "The person who is put right with God through faith shall live" (Romans 1:17). By faith, Martin Luther was put right with God! His followers were called *Protestants*. They explained their teaching by the saying, "Scripture alone, faith alone, grace alone." By *Scripture alone* they meant that the Bible, not tradition, should be the guide. By *faith alone,* they meant that people are made right with God by faith. Man could not do something to earn God's favor. By *grace alone,* they meant that people were put right with God by what Christ did on the cross. God gives freely to those who believe.

For You to Do

8 Why was revival needed?

....

9 List the three biblical teachings that Martin Luther restored.

....

....

....

Changes in Organization

Objective 5. *Describe several kinds of church organization.*

Luther wanted to return to biblical teachings. He also wanted biblical practice. Pagan practices were rejected. Idols were taken out of the churches. Men and women in the monasteries were sent out to work in the world. Protestants rejected or turned away from actions not found in the Bible. The leader of the church in the West rejected this movement. But Luther said, "We must obey the Bible rather than man!"

Protestants soon found they needed organization, too. Because each country had its own way of doing things, different kinds of organizations developed. Some Protestants wanted to keep the system they had known. They wanted a strong leader who told the area leaders what to do. The area leaders, in turn, told others. This is a form of organization with strong central leadership.

In Switzerland, where John Calvin led the Protestants, another form of organization developed. Switzerland had a long tradition of allowing its citizens to choose their own leaders. Church *organization* under Calvin allowed the people in the churches to choose their own leaders, who in turn chose area and national leaders. This form of *organization* gives more power to local leadership.

In other parts of Europe, another form of *organization* developed. These people wanted no authority beyond the local group of believers. They did not want a national leader nor contact with their kings. This form gives more power to each individual congregation.

Each group tried to find biblical support for its system. They all found some!

The New Testament does not say exactly what kind of organization a church should have. Organization should meet the need of the group. If a Christian feels that he is spiritual because he wants a certain kind of organization, he is wrong. This problem existed in the church at Corinth, too (1 Corinthians 1:12). The Corinthians found that the important part of church organization is harmony and love.

For You to Do

10 Circle the letter in front of each true statement.
 a Growing churches need organization.
 b There are several kinds of good organization.
 c Organization should meet the needs of the people.
 d Harmony and love are more important than the type of organization.

11 Does the New Testament teach one form of church government?

....

Find out what the church organization is like in your area. Does it serve to meet needs of your area? Fit into it and support it.

THE CHURCH IS REVIVED

From the time of Martin Luther's reformation, new revivals have come to the church. God has raised up new movements to teach from the Word truths that were not being taught. I do not have space enough to talk about all of these movements. Let me select just two.

Evangelical Movement

Objective 6. *Explain why revival was needed.*

At a time when church problems were great and morals were very low, God called a man to fit the situation. His name was John Wesley. In England, at that time, many people called themselves Christians. They had church membership but they were not true Christians. John Wesley preached that they must experience God. When there was no building to preach in, Wesley preached outside. He reached all classes of people with the gospel. He traveled by horse all over his country. He did more than preach. He wrote books, started schools, and helped those in need. He brought a spiritual change to the nation. There was less crime. Alcoholism disappeared in some areas. Families were strengthened.

For You to Do

12 Describe why revival was needed in Wesley's day.

....

....

Think about the spiritual needs in your area. Does your church need a revival? Pray that God will raise up a Christian like John Wesley for your area.

The History of the Church

Pentecostal Movement

Objective 7. *Describe what is different about the pentecostal movement.*

During the nineteenth century, the church sent out many people to preach in new areas. Missionaries from America and Europe established new churches in Africa, Asia, and on the islands of the sea.

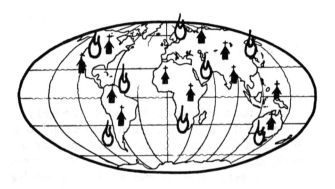

At the beginning of the twentieth century, God poured out His Holy Spirit on the church. It happened in many parts of the world at the same time. Many Christians experienced what the first disciples experienced at Pentecost. They received the gifts of the Spirit and the power to witness. This movement is known as the pentecostal movement. It has now spread around the world. Since about 1950, the experience has been reported in many different groups of believers. I believe that this movement is helping to prepare the church for the coming of Christ.

For You to Do

13 What is the spiritual experience for which the pentecostal movement is known?

....

Check your answers.

I hope this brief history of the church has helped you. Sometimes the story of the church is not a happy one. Sometimes the church has done things which did not glorify God. We must learn from the past. We must not repeat the same errors. We must also be understanding of Christians who belong to other groups. Organizations may differ, but we can all belong to Christ.

For the Christian, guidance does not only come from history, but from the whole Bible. In the next lesson, we will look at what the Bible says about the church. But before we leave this lesson, let us pray that God will use us to work in His church in our local area.

Check your Answers

13 Being filled with the Spirit.

1 a On Pentecost day.
  b There was a noise, and there were tongues of fire.
  c They were filled with the Holy Spirit and spoke in an unknown language.

12 There were church members who were not really believers. Morals were low.

2 Some made fun of the believers.

11 No. The Bible allows variety in church government.

3 He said, "Jesus whom you crucified is the one."

10 All these statements are true.

4 a They learned from the apostles.
  b They prayed together.
  c They had fellowship.
  e They ate together.

9 (In any order):
Faith alone.
Scripture alone.
Grace alone.

5 It grew.

8 Because there were many errors in teaching and practice.

6 b) so it could better provide help, protection, and unity.

7 c) The church forgot that it was supposed to minister to peoples' needs.

lesson 3 — what the church is

Jesus said, "I will build my church" (Matthew 16:18). What did He mean by the word *church?* What did His disciples understand by this word?

Perhaps you have noticed that the word *church* has been used many times in this study. It has been used in different ways. In Lesson 1, we used the term *church* to mean "God's people." In Lesson 2, we used the same word for the visible organization. Both ways are correct.

Many times we use a Bible word in everyday conversation. When we use a word in this way, we might not know its biblical meaning. Meanings depend on the *context,* or the setting in which the word is used. It is important to know what the word *church* means in the context of the Bible.

In this lesson, we will use the Bible. You will study a number of Scripture passages. In the last lesson, I did not mention that many people have given their lives to bring us the Bible. Not far from where I live, there is a stone sign on the spot where a man was put to death. His crime was wanting the Bible in the language of his people. God has protected His Word. Let us study it!

In this lesson you will study...

> The Meaning of the Word *Church*
> The Nature of the Church
> The Relationships of the Church

This lesson will help you...

- Understand the biblical meaning of the word *church*.
- Relate a local congregation to the universal church.
- Explain the supernatural nature of the church.

THE MEANING OF THE WORD *CHURCH*

Objective 1. *Define the word* church *in its Greek, Jewish, and Christian contexts.*

Greek was the language of the New Testament world. Paul wrote his letters to churches in the Greek language. What did the word *church* mean at that time? The word *church* meant "assembly." In Paul's time the word was made up of two small words. The two words together meant "called out." In Bible times, the word was used for an assembly of citizens called together. Citizens would meet to talk about some political or military problem. The word was also used of an army called together to fight. It could also be used to describe a law-making group. Today the word *church* sounds very religious. But in that time, the word was never used for a religious meeting.

For You to Do

1 Read about Paul's visit to Ephesus in Acts 19:23-41. The word *assembly* is found in verses 32, 39, and 41. What kind of assembly was this? Write the words your Bible uses instead of *church* or *assembly*.

a Verse 32 ....
b Verse 39 ....
c Verse 41 ....

What the Church Is

2 Which of these definitions are NOT the Greek meaning of the word *assembly*?
a) A political gathering
b) An army called together
c) A religious meeting
d) An assembly of citizens

As you know, the Bible is divided into two main parts: the Old and New Testaments. In the Old Testament, the Jews were called God's people. Many Jews, like Abraham and David, believed God and obeyed Him. Their life stories are in the Old Testament. We learn much from reading about their lives.

In Jesus' day, however, many Jews did not obey God. They did not study His Word. To help these people, a special translation of the Old Testament was made. The word *church*, or *assembly*, was used almost 100 times in this version. Sometimes it was used for secular (not religious) gatherings, and at other times it was used for religious meetings. From the time Christians started using the word *church*, the Jews stopped using it. A gathering of Christians was a church. A meeting of Jews was called a *synagogue*. Jews who believed in Jesus were often put out of the synagogue. (See John 9:22 for one example.)

For You to Do

3 The word *church* was used by the Jews to mean
a) a religious meeting.
b) a secular gathering.
c) either religious or secular meetings.

4 An example of the use of the word is also found in Acts 7:38. Stephen, a Jew who became a Christian, used this word. Who were in the "assembly" (church) in the desert? Read Acts 7:38, and write your answer.

....

The word *church* can be found more than 100 times in the New Testament. It can be found in almost every book. When Christians called their meetings "the church" or "the assembly," they did not mean a political or military meeting. They did not mean a meeting of the Jewish people, although many of the early Christians were Jewish! They meant *the people who were called out by God.* They meant the company of people saved by faith in Jesus Christ. I will explain more about this Christian usage throughout this course.

For You to Do

5 What do Christians mean by the word *church*?

....

THE NATURE OF THE CHURCH

Objective 2. *Relate the local congregation to the universal church.*

The word *church* means a local assembly of all those who have faith in Christ. Often in the New Testament it means a certain church. See, for example, Paul's greeting "to the people of the church in Thessalonica" (1 Thessalonians 1:1). Sometimes the Bible refers to several such gatherings in a certain area. An example is, "the churches in Judea" (Galatians 1:22).

At other times, the word *church* is used to mean something bigger. It means the *universal* church. It is not the assembly, or meeting, but those *belonging* to the assembly. (See Acts 8:1-3.) When believers suffered and were scattered, they were still a part of the church. In Matthew 16:18, Jesus is speaking of building the *universal* church, the body of believers in Christ, all over the world.

So we see that the church is not made up of people from just one race, but from *all* races. The church is not people from one nation, but from *all* nations. In Galatians 3:28 we read:

> So there is no difference between Jews and Gentiles, between slaves and free men, between men and women; you are all one in union with Christ Jesus.

For You to Do

6 Study each of the following passages. Decide whether it refers to a local assembly or to the universal church.

a 1 Corinthians 4:17 ....
....

b 2 Thessalonians 1:1 ....
....

c Colossians 1:18 ....
....

d Ephesians 3:8-10 ....
....

e Ephesians 3:20-21 ....
....

f 2 Corinthians 11:8 ....
....

What the Church Is 45

7 How is the local church related to the universal church? ....

....

THE RELATIONSHIPS OF THE CHURCH

Objective 3. *Explain the relationship of the church to each member of the Trinity (The Father, The Son, and the Holy Spirit).*

As we have seen, in Bible times the word church was not a religious word. How did believers refer to the church?

The early Christians called the church a name in their language (*ekklesia*) which means the congregation or the *assembly of God*. The people were called by God. It was God's assembly. Paul wrote "to the people of the church in Thessalonica, who belong to God the Father and the Lord Jesus Christ" (1 Thessalonians 1:1). In the same way, he wrote "To the church of God which is in Corinth, to all who are called to be God's holy people, who belong to him in union with Christ Jesus, together with all people everywhere who worship our Lord Jesus Christ, their Lord and ours" (1 Corinthians 1:2).

For You To Do

8 Each of the following verses tells us who the church belongs to. Read each verse. Then write the description of the church found in each passage.

a 2 Thessalonians 1:1 ....

....

b Galatians 1:13 ....

....

c 1 Corinthians 11:16 ....

....

◻ ◻ ◻ ◻ ◻

The church is called forth by God and called unto Jesus Christ. To the church at Corinth Paul wrote, "God (the Father) is to be trusted, the God who called you to have fellowship with His Son Jesus Christ, our Lord (1 Corinthians 1:9). At times the church is called "of Christ." (See, for example, Romans 16:16.) Jesus said, "I will build my church" (Matthew 16:18). Paul spoke of Christ Who "is himself the Savior of the church" (Ephesians 5:23). Then he added, "Christ loved the church and gave his life for it" (Ephesians 5:25).

Believers are spoken of as "in Christ." Christians are identified with Christ in his death (Romans 6:6). It is because we are "in Christ" that we suffer (Romans 8:17; 2 Timothy 2:12).

What the Church Is 47

For You to Do

9 Read again Romans 8:17 and 2 Timothy 2:12. What promise is made to those who suffer "in Christ"? ....

10 Answer the following questions, each with one word.

   a Who calls forth the church? ....

   b Believers are in ....

The Holy Spirit gives the church its supernatural (spiritual) nature. Because of the Spirit, the church is unlike any human assembly. The church is seen where the Holy Spirit is known. The power, or life, of the church is not human, but spiritual.

For You to Do

11 Study each of the following passages. Write what the Holy Spirit does for the church.
   a Philippians 2:1 ....

   b Acts 1:8 ....

   c 1 Corinthians 12:8-12 ....

   d Ephesians 4:3-4 ....

Check your answer.

We must praise God that He has called us to be part of His *church*. The church is called forth by God, identified with Christ, and filled with the Spirit. God's church is both local and universal. Believers everywhere love the same Christ. They "have all been given the one Spirit to drink" (1 Corinthians 12:13).

What is the church? It is the supernatural fellowship of believers. God planned it from the beginning. It has shown itself continually since the New Testament days. It is God's witness in your area and your country.

What the Church Is

Check your Answers

11 a The Spirit gives fellowship.
  b The Spirit gives power for witness.
  c The Spirit gives spiritual gifts.
  d The Spirit provides unity.

1 a The meeting.
  b A legal meeting.
  c The meeting.

10 a God (the Father).
  b Christ.

2 c) A religious meeting.

9 They will rule with Christ.

3 c) either religious or secular meetings.

8 a "church ... who belong to God our Father and the Lord Jesus Christ."
  b "church of God"
  c "churches of God"

4 The people of Israel.

7 Christians who make up the local church are a part of the body of Christ, or the universal church.

5 The company of believers.

6 a Local *(every church)*.
  b Local *(the people of the church in Thessalonica)*.
  c Universal *(He is the head of the body, the church)*.
  d Universal *(by means of the church)*.
  e Universal *(glory in the church)*.
  f Local *(paid by the other churches)*.

lesson 4
how I can be a part of God's church

We have studied much about the church's past. We have seen how God has been working out His plan. We have also studied the meaning of the word *church*. So now we are ready to look at the present. We do not live in the past. We do not live in a world of ideas. We live today.

What does the past mean to me? What does the meaning of the *church* matter to me? In this lesson we will look at the church and at *you*. This is a very personal lesson. It might be the most important part of this book. Many people have problems because they do not know the truth presented in this lesson. The church has many troubles when it does not understand the truth. Study these pages carefully.

Probably I have never met you, and you have never seen me. But if you have accepted the Lord Jesus Christ as your Savior, then we are both members of the church. By God's grace, someday we will meet. We will be together in heaven! In heaven we will praise God together for His grace in Christ. We will understand more completely the nature of His church.

In this lesson you will study...

Man's Responsibility
God's Work in Salvation
God's Names for His People

This lesson will help you...

- List three things man must do to become part of God's church.
- Explain what God does to make people a part of His church.
- Use properly four biblical terms for believers.

MAN'S RESPONSIBILITY

Objective 1. *Explain the biblical meaning of the words* repentance, conversion, *and* belief.

Repentance

We have seen some of the wonderful things God will do for His church. It would be terrible to be left out. What must you do to be part of God's church?

First, the Bible tells us that we must *repent*. To repent means "to change your mind, your way of thinking, and your attitude." In repenting, a man looks at his past. He *feels sorry* for his errors and decides to change. Repentance is moving "self" from the center and giving that place to God. Paul described it this way, "But all those things that I might count as profit I now reckon as loss for Christ's sake" (Philippians 3:7). Jesus told a wonderful story about a young man who left his father and wasted his money and his life. Then he repented and returned to his father. He felt sorry for what he had done, and decided to change his life. That is true repentance (Luke 15:11-32).

How I Can Be a Part of God's Church

For You to Do

1 Read each of the passages below. Write the main topic of each of these Scriptures.

a Matthew 3:2 ....

b Matthew 4:17 ....

c Acts 2:38 ....

2 Write the definition of the word *repent* in your own words.

....

Conversion

The word *conversion* is found 40 times in the New Testament. It means "the act of turning." It is used many times in the book of Acts. These words are usually followed by "to the Lord" or "to God" (Acts 9:35; 11:21; 15:19). A person must turn *from* the old (repentance) and *towards* the new (conversion). He must give himself to God.

This turning is both *away from* something and *towards* something else. Paul told the church at Thessalonica that Christians everywhere "speak about how you received us when we visited you, and how you turned away from idols to God, to serve the true and living God" (1 Thessalonians 1:9).

For You to Do

3 Answer the following questions:

a What does *conversion* mean? ....
....

b From what must man turn away? ....
....

c To whom must man turn ....

Belief

To *believe in* means "to put trust in" or "to count on." The Bible says, "Abraham put his trust in the Lord, and because of this the Lord was pleased with him and accepted him" (Genesis 15:6). The New Testament quotes these words, but it adds, "the Scripture predicted that God would put the Gentiles right with himself through faith." Faith and belief are very similar in meaning.

How I Can Be a Part of God's Church   55

To have belief in Christ is to meet Him, to love Him, to trust Him. It means to obey Him and to remain faithful to Him. Faith is not inactive. Faith is *active* trust in God. Our faith is shown by our actions.

For You to Do

4 A jailer asked Paul and Silas, "Sirs, what must I do to be saved?" Write your answer to this question. Then, read Acts 16:30-31 to find the answer given.

....

....

5 Define *belief* in your own words.

....

Repentance, conversion, and belief are closely related. They are three parts of the same experience. Have you truly repented, been converted, and do you have faith (belief) in Christ? If you have not done so, accept Christ by faith now. This is the only way into God's church.

GOD'S WORK IN SALVATION

So far in this lesson, I have shown you man's part in coming to God. Yet man cannot do his part without God's help. God brings people into the church. Luke said of the church, "And every day the Lord added to their group those who were being saved" (Acts 2:47).

The New Birth

Objective 2. *Describe what happens when the new birth takes place in a person's life.*

It is not by physical birth that people become Christians. It is by the *new birth*. Speaking to Nicodemus, Jesus made clear the need for being born again. (See John 3:3-7.) Jesus said, "A person is born physically of human parents, but he is born spiritually of the Spirit" (John 3:6). Paul repeated the same truth, "What is made of flesh and blood cannot share in God's kingdom" (1 Corinthians 15:50).

How I Can Be a Part of God's Church

Yes, God wants you to be born again. He wants you to have a new start. The Bible calls this *regeneration.* Just as you were born into a human family, you must be born spiritually into God's family.

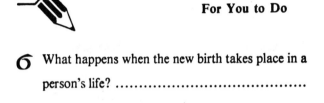

For You to Do

6 What happens when the new birth takes place in a person's life? ....
....

The New Nature

Objective 3. *Define the new nature.*

You were born with a certain nature. When you are born again, you get a new nature. You get God's nature. Peter spoke of the believer as one who "came to share the divine nature" (2 Peter 1:4).

Paul explained it this way, "When anyone is joined to Christ, he is a new being; the old is gone, the new has come" (2 Corinthians 5:17). The Bible teaches that there are two evidences of being born again. The first evidence is the witness of the Holy Spirit in our hearts (Romans 8:16). The second is the *fruit of righteousness* which is produced in the believer's life.

They who are born of the Spirit should bring forth fruit of the Spirit. (See Galatians 5:22-23 for a list of the fruit of the Spirit.)

For You to Do

7 Read Matthew 12:33-35 and explain the new nature.

....

8 Examine your life and answer these questions with *yes* or *no*.

  a Do you have the witness of the Holy Spirit in your heart? ....

  b Can people see the fruit of the Spirit in your life? ....

If you answered *no* to these questions, perhaps you should re-examine your life to be sure that you have repented, turned from sin, and are trusting completely in God.

GOD'S NAMES FOR HIS PEOPLE

Objective 4. *List and define four biblical terms for believers.*

Many people call themselves Christians. Some of these people, however, have not had the spiritual experience we have studied. They are not really

Christians even if they associate with the visible church. They are not members of God's true church. They are called "unconverted" people.

Unconverted people who associate with the visible church cannot be called by any of the names given in the Bible to members of the true church. We will look at only four of these names. But our list could be much longer.

Disciples

Throughout the book of Acts, believers are called *disciples*. (See Acts 6:2; 9:1; 11:26; 14:21-22; 18:27; and 19:9 [KJV].) Jesus called His followers disciples. A disciple is a learner. He adopts the doctrine of his master. In the gospels, the disciples stayed close to the Master. They bound themselves to obey Christ.

Unconverted people cannot obey Christ. Unconverted people cannot be called disciples. Such people should not be called Christians, because they are not true Christians.

Saint

The New Testament often calls church members *saints*. (See Acts 9:13, 41; 2 Corinthians 1:1; 13:13; Ephesians 4:12; and Colossians 1:12 [KJV].) Notice that saints are on earth as well as in heaven.

Saints are those separated unto God. Unconverted people are not saints. Unconverted people are not in God's church. They have not been set apart for God.

Brethren

The term *brethren* is the most common name for believers in the New Testament. This word shows the ties between believers within the church. The church is God's family. Believers have been born into God's family by the new birth. Believers are Christ's brethren (Romans 8:29; Hebrews 2:11-12, 17 [KJV]).

Unconverted people are not Christ's brethren. They are not, therefore, part of God's church.

Christians

As we have seen, believers were not at first called *Christians*. They were called disciples, saints, or brethren. The term *Christian* was first used to mock believers. But it refers to those that belong to Him. They are like Christ (Acts 11:26; 26:28; and I Peter 4:16).

How I Can Be a Part of God's Church

The term *Christian* should only be used for those who have been born again and have Christ's nature.

The early believers were called by many names. Each name, however, is to be used only for born-again people in the church. They should not be used for those who associate with a visible church organization but have not been born again.

For You to Do

9 We have studied four Bible terms which describe a believer. List them here.

....
....
....
....

10 From the Bible terms which describe a believer, select one to fit each of the following definitions.

a A learner who is very close to his master:

....

b A term used to mock believers because they acted like Christ: ....

c Means "separated to God": ....

d Shows that all believers are part of God's family: ....

I trust that you have had the experience of being born again. I trust you are part of God's church. This experience is the most important thing in your life. You might be a church member. You might be called a Christian. But you *must* be born again to be part of God's church. Do it right now!

Now that you have completed the first four lessons, you are ready to answer the first section of your student report. Review Lessons 1-4, then follow the instructions in your student report for filling out the answer sheet. Then return your answer sheet to the address given on the last page of the student report.

Check Your Answers

10 a Disciple.
   b Christian.
   c Saint.
   d Brethren.

1 a Repentance.
  b Repentance.
  c Repentance.

9 Disciples, saints, brethren, Christians.

2 Your own words, but it should include the idea of feeling sorry and wanting to change.

8 Your answer. If your answer is *no*, or if you are not sure, pray and ask God to give you the new nature.

3 a The act of turning.
  b From idols, sin, etc.
  c God.

7 People, like trees, give fruit according to their nature. At the new birth, believers get a new nature.

4 "Believe in the Lord Jesus Christ and you will be saved."

6 He is born into God's family. It is a *spiritual* birth.

5 Your own words, but it should include the ideas of trust in, rely upon.

lesson 5
how the church is like a body

Only believers are true members of God's church. In the last lesson, we saw that believers are called many names. They are called disciples, saints, brethren, and Christians. Each name tells us something about them.

In the same way, the church is called different names. Each name tells us something about the church. We will look at one of these names. The Bible often says the church is like a body. In this lesson, we will learn what that means.

In the church, you have contact with other believers. They are important to you. Thank God for these people. Ask God what you can do to help them. They can help you, also. This study is wasted unless you apply the information to your own life. Put into practice today what you learn.

In this lesson you will study...

Christ and the Church
    Christ the Source of Life
    Christ the Lord
    Christ the Provider
Relationships Within the Church
    Unity in the Church
    Variety in the Church
    Caring in the Church

This lesson will help you...

- Describe how the church is similar to a living body.
- Explain the relationship of the church to Christ.
- Describe the relationships within the church.
- Find your responsibility to others in the church.

CHRIST AND THE CHURCH

Objective 1. *Explain where the church gets its spiritual life.*

The Bible compares the church to many things. It says the church is like a building (Ephesians 2:21), a wife (Ephesians 5:22-23), a flock (John 10:16), and a vine (John 15:4). This list is not complete. It could be much longer. Someone has counted more than 200 such pictures of the church in the New Testament!

We cannot study all of these. I have chosen one. The Bible says the church is like a *body*. We will learn much as we study this comparison.

Christ the Source of Life

A living body is growing and active. Each body has a head. The relationship between the head and the body is very important. Paul wrote to the church at Colossae, "He [Christ] is the head of his body, the church; he is the source of the body's life" (Colossians 1:18). The church takes its life from Christ. Buildings, organization, and meetings do not bring life. Only Jesus can do that.

How the Church is Like a Body

Each believer, and the whole church, have "been given full life in union with him" (Colossians 2:10). The body is identified with the head. The church is identified with Christ.

For You to Do

1 Choose the best answer of each two given in parentheses, and write it in the blank space.

a The church lives because it draws life from

....
(its organization) (Christ)

b Who is the head of the church?

....
(the bride) (Christ)

2 Read Colossians 2:12-13 and complete the following sentence.

Believers are identified with Christ in His

.... and in His ....

Christ the Lord

Objective 2. *Name the head of the church.*

Christ is not only the source of life. He is also the Lord of the church. Just as a wife obeys her husband, the church obeys Christ (Ephesians 5:24). The hand does not tell the head what to do—the head tells the hand. The church must be obedient to Christ. "God put all things under Christ's feet and gave him to the church as supreme Lord over all things. The church is Christ's body, the completion of him who himself completes all things everywhere" (Ephesians 1:22-23).

Everybody has a lord. Some people obey a human master. Many obey sin. The message of the early Christians was "Jesus Christ is Lord!"

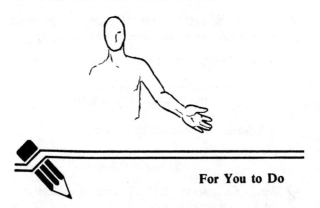

For You to Do

3 Choose the best answer of each two given in parentheses, and write it in the blank.

a The Lord of the church is

....
(an official) (Christ)

b The head of the church is

....
(a man) (Christ)

Christ the Provider

Objective 3. *Explain how Christ is the church's provider.*

Jesus Christ is a loving Lord. We give ourselves to Him. In love, Christ takes care of us. Paul explained, "No one ever hates his own body. Instead, he feeds it and takes care of it, just as Christ does the church; for we are members of his body" (Ephesians 5:29-30). The church lives because of its contact with Christ. It grows because of Christ. It is cared for by Christ. "Under Christ's control the whole body is nourished and held together by its joints and ligaments, and it grows as God wants it to grow" (Colossians 2:19).

For You to Do

4 Think of some of the ways Christ has provided for the church in your area. List them here.

....
....

5 List the three ways that Christ is related to His body, the church.

....

....

....

RELATIONSHIPS WITHIN THE CHURCH

Unity in the Church

Objective 4. *Explain the unity of the body.*

The New Testament is written more to the church as a whole rather than to individual believers. Christians cannot live away from other believers. In the early church, new converts were quickly taken into the fellowship. Luke wrote, "The group of believers was one in mind and heart" (Acts 4:32).

Regardless of race, nationality, or social standing, all believers are united in one church. "There is one body and one Spirit" (Ephesians 4:4). This unity does not mean that all Christians must belong to the same church organization. It does not mean that all believers

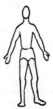

How the Church is Like a Body

must worship in the same way. It does mean, however, that there should be a spirit of love and oneness among believers.

Divisions in the church are never good. They are painful. The church suffers because of them. The church at Corinth had this problem. (See 1 Corinthians 1:12-13.) Paul appeals for unity. "And so there is no division in the body, but all its different parts have the same concern for one another" (1 Corinthians 12:25). Divisions in the church usually are caused by people having a greater concern for themselves than for others.

For You to Do

6 Choose the best answer of each two given in parentheses and write it in the blank.
a Biblical unity means the same

....
(organization) (spirit)

b Church divisions are usually caused by

....
(selfishness) (love)

Variety in the Church

Objective 5. *Identify your own gifts in the body.*

Unity does not mean that every Christian is exactly the same. No! Every Christian is different. Variety gives strength and balance. "Christ is like a single body, which has many parts; it is still one body, even though it is made up of different parts" (1 Corinthians 12:12).

One part of the body cannot say to another part, "I don't need you!" Every part needs every other part. Christians need each other. (See 1 Corinthians 12:12-26.) Believers may differ in what they do (v. 17), in strength (v. 22), and honor (v. 23). But there is only one body. Paul explained this same truth to the church at Rome: "Though we are many, we are one body in union with Christ, and we are all joined to each other as different parts of one body. So we are to use our different gifts in accordance with the grace that God has given us" (Romans 12:5-6).

For You to Do

7 In Romans 12:6-8 is a list of some of the gifts that God has given to the body. Read through the list, then put an **X** by gifts which you have used by God's grace.

a Speak God's message ....
b Serve ....

How the Church is Like a Body 73

    c Teach ....
    d Encourage others ....
    e Share ....
    f Use authority ....
    g Show kindness ....

8 Now notice how each of the gifts should be used. How are you to use the gifts that you have? Pray about this matter.

Caring in the Church

Objective 6. *Describe how believers can care for one another.*

You have a part in God's church. You will accept this seriously, as a service to Christ. Part of your responsibility is to care for other believers. As we have seen, in the body the hand needs the ear and the ear needs the foot. As the Bible says, "Under his [Christ's] control all the different parts of the body fit together, and the whole body is held together by every joint with which it is provided (Ephesians 4:16). No part of the body can get along by itself. Every part needs every other part.

Part of this relationship is truthfulness. "Everyone must tell the truth to his fellow believer, because we are all members together in the body of Christ" (Ephesians 4:25). Because we are fellow believers, we must help each other. "Help to carry one another's burden" (Galatians 6:2). Paul speaks this same way about suffering. "If one part of the body suffers, all the other parts suffer with it; if one part is praised, all the other parts share its happiness" (1 Corinthians 12:26). The care for others is the mark of the church. John wrote, "If you have love for one another, then everyone will know that you are my disciples" (John 13:35).

For You to Do

9 Look over this section. List ways that you can express care for others. Do you do all of these?

....
....
....

10 Review this lesson. Ask God to help you find and fulfill your part in the body. Write below the things you need to start doing as your part in the body of Christ.

....
....
....

How the Church is Like a Body 75

Check Your Answers

10 Your answer. Ask God to help you.

1 a Christ.
   b Christ.

9 Telling the truth.
   Helping with burdens.
   Suffering with others.
   Rejoicing with others.
   Loving others.

2 death, resurrection.

8 Your answer.

3 Christ.
   Christ.

7 Your list should have a number of items marked with an **X**. Ask God to use you in the ministry of spiritual gifts to the body.

4 Your answer, but maybe things like good leadership, opportunities to witness, unity, etc.

6 a spirit.
   b selfishness.

5 Christ is the source of life.
   Christ is Lord
   Christ is the provider.

lesson 6
what the church does for itself

In the last lesson we saw how the church is like a body. We saw that people can be different from each other and still have unity. We finished the lesson by considering what we can do for others.

This lesson carries on the same theme. We have a duty to other believers. If we do not share with others, or strengthen others, we are hurting them. We can *rob* them of the help they need. This lesson should help you to do your part in the body of Christ.

This lesson is personal. It is for you to apply. You must find and do your duty. You might learn a great deal about the church. But it does not profit you or others if you do not apply what you learn. Ask God to help you do this.

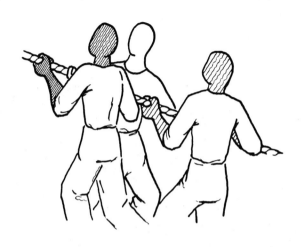

In this lesson you will study...

The Sharing Church
The Strengthening Church
The Sanctifying Church

This lesson will help you...

- Describe three ways believers help each other.
- Find your responsibility to others.

THE SHARING CHURCH

Objective 1. *List ways you can practice biblical fellowship.*

The first Christians "spent their time in learning from the apostles, taking part in the fellowship, and sharing in the fellowship meals and prayers" (Acts 2:42).

The word *fellowship* means "friendship, helping, and sharing." This sharing is deep and personal.

When Paul was in prison, he did not have this fellowship. I believe he missed it. In his letter to the church at Philippi, Paul talks much about *fellowship*. He speaks of fellowship in the gospel (Philippians 1:5), fellowship with the Spirit (2:1), fellowship in suffering (3:10), fellowship in trouble (4:14), and fellowship in giving (4:15).

For You to Do

1 Look over this discussion of fellowship. Make a

list the ways that the early Christians had fellowship.

....

....

2 Make another list. This time list ways that you can help others through fellowship. Be specific. Use the names of those Christians who need help. Write your list in your notebook.

THE STRENGTHENING CHURCH

Objective 2. *Describe ways you can practice biblical edification.*

The terms *fellowship* and *edify* are related. The first term stresses the idea of "being together." The second word means "to build or to strengthen." Believers are not only to be together, they are also to help each other.

Although believers are responsible to build themselves up in faith (Jude 20), they must also build up others. When Christians meet, each has something to do to help. Although each one is different, "Everything must be of help to the church" (1 Corinthians 14:26).

This process of building up is never finished. Peter warned, "Be on your guard . . . but continue to grow in the grace and knowledge of our Lord and Savior Jesus Christ" (2 Peter 3:17-18).

Speaking of the church, Paul said "each one must be careful how he builds" (1 Corinthians 3:10).

Sometimes Christians try to build the church by pride or ambition. These are the things that Paul calls "wood or grass or straw" (v. 12). Each man's work will be tested.

How can believers help to build up the church? The Bible suggests some answers. One way is by working for peace in the church. "So then, we must aim at those things that bring peace and that help to strengthen one another" (Romans 14:19). Another way is by encouragement. "And so encourage one another and help one another, just as you are now doing" (1 Thessalonians 5:11). Another is by love. "So when each separate part works as it should, the whole body grows and builds itself up through love" (Ephesians 4:16). Perhaps the best way is to reflect, or be like Christ. "Keep your roots deep in him, build your lives on him and become stronger in your faith" (Colossians 2:7).

For You to Do

3 Study Ephesians 4:11-16 and answer the following questions:
a What contrast does Paul make in verse 13?

....

What the Church Does for Itself

    b How many times do the words *grow* and *build* appear?

....

    c Why does Christ give the gifts (v. 11) to the church?

....

4 We have looked at the list of gifts in Romans 12:6-8. Now let us look at another list. It is from 1 Corinthians 12:28. Read through this list, then put an X by the gifts God has given your church.

...... Apostles	...... Healing ministries
...... Prophets	...... Leadership
...... Teachers	...... Helping others
...... Miracles	...... Speak in another language given by the Holy Spirit

5 In prayer, ask God what you can do to build up the church. Ask Him if you have kept the church from growing. Let us promise to help the church.

THE SANCTIFYING CHURCH

Objective 3. *Define the word sanctification and explain our responsibility in this.*

The word *sanctify* is related to the word *saint*. It means "to be set apart for God." Those who have been *sanctified* have been set apart for God. They have been called out. They are to be holy just as God is holy (1 Peter 1:16). The church is called a "holy temple" (Ephesians 2:21). The Holy Spirit has been poured out upon the church (1 John 2:20).

In one sense, the church is perfect in Christ. In another sense, it is moving to perfection. Sanctification is not a single experience nor a ceremony. It is Christ preparing the church. As the letter to the church at Ephesus says:

> Husbands, love your wives just as Christ loved the church and gave his life for it. He did this to dedicate the church to God by his word, after making it clean by washing it in water, in order to present the church to himself in all its beauty, pure and faultless, without spot or wrinkle or any other imperfection (Ephesians 5:25-27).

The Bible says we should do all we can to make ourselves pure, or clean (without sin). "So, then, let us purify ourselves from everything that makes body or soul unclean, and let us be completely holy by living in reverence for God" (2 Corinthians 7:1).

On the other hand, it is God who purifies us. The truth is that if we judge ourselves we will not be condemned by the Lord. This means that if we examine our lives and correct sinful actions, God will not condemn us for those actions.

In 1 Corinthians 11:31-32 we read:

> If we would examine ourselves first, we would not come under God's judgment. But we are judged and punished by the Lord, so that we shall not be condemned together with the world.

For You to Do

6 Choose the best answer of each two given in parentheses and write it in the blank.

a Sanctification is ....
(a ceremony) (a continuing process)

b Who purifies believers?

....
(Only the Lord)
(Both the believer and the Lord)

I have a daughter. Sometimes she does not do what is right and I must correct her. I want to help her learn what is right. This is also true with God. As His son, I know that He corrects me. I do not enjoy correction, but I know it is best for me.

Hebrews 12:5-11 tells us that God's correction should be an encouragement. It teaches us to respect God our Father (v. 9). It is for our good and our growth in holiness (v. 10). Therefore, we should submit to God's correction.

If our brothers or sisters in Christ do something wrong, we should try to help them. We should not talk about them to others, but speak to them individually. We should love others and try to treat them just as we know God treats each of us.

Sometimes unbelievers will not accept Christ because they see sin in the church. This should not be! Paul applied Christ's instruction on this matter to the church at Corinth. (See 1 Corinthians 5:6-8, 13.) Every believer must do his part to keep the church free from sin.

For You to Do

7 Choose the best answer of each two given in parentheses and write it in the blank.

a Fellowship means ....
 (sharing) (to make holy)

b Edify means ....
 (to build up) (to make holy)

c The church is being prepared as a bride for

....
 (its own beauty) (Christ)

d If a believer sins, you have the responsibility to

....
 (tell others about it) (talk to him alone)

8 Look back over this lesson. Notice your answers to questions 2 and 4. Now is the time to use your

What the Church Does for Itself

gifts for the church. Remember that Christ loved the church. Ask God to give you that same love for the "body of Christ." Then it will be easy to share, to build up, and to help others be sanctified.

Check Your Answers

8 After you have done this, you are ready for the next lesson.

1 Your list may be different from mine but I listed:
in prayer
in meals
in travel
in helping
in sharing during trouble

7 a sharing.
  b to build up.
  c Christ.
  d talk to him alone.

2 Your own answer.

6 a a continuing process.
  b Both the believer and the Lord.

3 a A contrast between babies and mature people.
  b Four (in *Today's English Version*).
  c To help it grow.

5 Your prayer.

4 Your list should contain several **X**'s.

lesson 7: what the church does for the world

In the last lesson, we saw that believers have responsibilities to other believers. All believers are part of God's family. Christians have a special contact with brothers and sisters in Christ.

But the church also has a duty to non-believers. A Christian must never be so concerned about other believers that he forgets about those outside the church. In this lesson, we will look at the believer's duty to unbelievers.

Like other lessons in this study, you must apply what you learn. God is not pleased if we know what to do, but do not do it. Just as James said, "The person who does not do the good he knows he should do is guilty of sin" (James 4:17). Let us apply this lesson by doing the things we are taught.

In this lesson you will study...

Believers Oppose Evil
Believers Announce the Gospel
Believers Send Workers
Believers Support Workers

This lesson will help you...

- List three things a Christian should do to reach unbelievers.
- Define the word *evangelize*.
- Find your responsibility in reaching the lost.

BELIEVERS OPPOSE EVIL

Objective 1. *Explain how the believer can oppose evil.*

Have you ever owed someone a certain amount of money? Sometimes we owe a debt which money cannot pay. We have a responsibility which money cannot fulfill. Every believer has such a debt. What is this obligation? Paul expressed it. "I want to win converts among you also, as I have among other Gentiles. For I have an obligation to all peoples, to the civilized and to the savage, to the educated and to the ignorant" (Romans 1:13-14).

Godly people should be known by their godly actions. God's people should do good works. Jesus said, "You are like salt for all mankind" (Matthew 5:13). But if salt does not do what it is supposed to do, it is worthless. Jesus also said, "You are like light for the whole world" (Matthew 5:14). But a light should not be hidden—it should shine. A light shines upon everyone in a room. "In the same way your light must shine before people, so that they will see the good things you do and praise your Father in heaven" (Matthew 5:16).

When a person becomes a Christian, he begins a new life. He no longer does the evil things he used to do. He wants to do those things which please God. Just as salt changes the taste of food, and light changes darkness, the Christian's godly life has an influence on those around him. He influences others to do good. In this way, he is a force against evil.

What the Church Does for the World 89

I once read the life story of a young man named Nicky. Nicky hated everyone. He had learned to fight and to kill. His friends formed a gang to steal and destroy. Nicky started using drugs. Before Nicky was out of his teenage years, his life was very ungodly. But, one day, someone told him about God's love. A Christian told Nicky that he could have a new life in Christ Jesus. Nicky accepted Christ. He quit his gang. He stopped fighting and killing. But Nicky did more than that! He started helping other young people who had similar problems. He told them about Jesus Christ. He helped them give up their drugs and stop hating people.

By God's grace, evil was defeated in Nicky's life. But more than that, Nicky used his influence to stop evil. Nicky's life was like a light shining into the darkness of a sinful community.

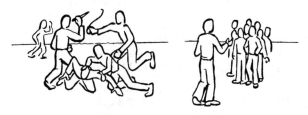

Christians can restrain evil by their prayers, also. Abraham's nephew, Lot, did not love God as Abraham did. Abraham, of course, was very concerned about his nephew. He tried to encourage Lot to serve God, but Lot wanted to live in a city which was known for its sinfulness. Abraham prayed for his nephew. Because of Abraham's prayers, God saved Lot from being destroyed with the wicked city. You should read Abraham's prayer in Genesis 18:22-33.

For You to Do

1 Fill in the blank with the correct word.

a Believers fight against evil by doing

....

b Jesus compared Christians to

....

and ....
c The things that happened to Nicky show that a

Christian can fight against ....
in the area where he lives.
d The life of Abraham shows that those who love

God should ....
for those who do not love God.

BELIEVERS ANNOUNCE THE GOSPEL

Objective 2. *Define the word* evangelize.

Paul wrote to the church at Philippi concerning the duties of Christians: "Be innocent and pure as God's perfect children, who live in a world of corrupt and sinful people. You must shine among them like stars lighting the sky, as you offer them the message of life" (Philippians 2:15-16).

Paul says it is not enough just to live a godly life. We

What the Church Does for the World

must also "offer them the message of life." The gospel must be told in deed, but also in words!

Jesus said, "Go, then, to all peoples everywhere and make them my disciples" (Matthew 28:19). This passage is often called *The Great Commission*. Mark records a similar passage, "Go throughout the whole world and preach the gospel to all mankind" (Mark 16:15). Here the word *preach* does not mean a formal speech before a group. It means simply to *tell* or *announce*. Not every believer can *preach* but every Christian can tell the gospel. Often the word *evangelize* is used. This word means "to announce the good news." Every believer must obey Christ's words to announce the gospel and make disciples.

As we learned in the last lesson, God wants His body, the church, to grow. "It grows as God wants it to grow" (Colossians 2:19). The early church was a growing church. Three thousand people were added to the church in a single day (Acts 2:41). Growth is normal for the body of Christ. "And every day the Lord added to their group those who were being saved" (Acts 2:47). A church which is not growing is not a healthy church.

For You to Do

2 Choose the best answer of each two given in parentheses, and write it in the blank.

a In Matthew 28:19, the word *preach* means

....
(give a sermon)/(tell the gospel)

b The word *evangelize* means

....
(announce the good news) (preach)

c A church which does not grow by winning people to Christ is ....
(a healthy church) (an unhealthy church)

3 What are you doing to fulfill the great commission? When were new believers added to your group? Make a list of those to whom you should speak about Christ. Pray for each one. Speak to each one.

....
....

4 Look back over this lesson and list two duties of the church.

a ....

b ....

BELIEVERS SEND WORKERS

Objective 3. *Explain why workers must be sent out by the church.*

The church must tell the good news. In Matthew 28:19 and Mark 16:15, we find the word *go*. Sometimes you do not need to go far. But other times, Christians need to go to a different area. The gospel must be told in areas where there are no believers. Jesus said, "The message about repentance and the forgiveness of sins must be preached to all nations" (Luke 24:47). (The word *nations* here means tribes or groups of people.) The church has a large task. But God has promised us His Holy Spirit. "But when the Holy Spirit comes upon you, you will be filled with power, and you will be witnesses for me" (Acts 1:8).

The early church obeyed by sending out workers.

> In the church at Antioch there were some prophets and teachers .... While they were serving the Lord and fasting, the Holy Spirit said to them, "Set apart Barnabas and Saul, to do the work to which I have called them." They fasted and prayed, placed their hands on them, and sent them off (Acts 13:1-3).

This passage gives us a model to follow. I will list some of the principles shown in this passage.

1. The men who were sent were faithful in a ministry in their home church.
2. The decision was made after much prayer.
3. The men felt the call of God, and the church sent them.

The workers were sent by God and by the church. After the workers returned, they reported to the church. "When they arrived in Antioch, they gathered the people of the church together and told them about all that God had done with them" (Acts 14:27).

For You to Do

5 Circle the letter in front of the correct answer to this question. When Jesus said, "Go and tell the good news," He meant
a) go to all my neighbors who are living nearby.
b) go a great distance in order to spread the gospel in foreign lands.
c) go to those who have not heard the good news, whether nearby or far away.

6 Circle the letter in front of the correct answer to this question. Sending of workers is something which is done by the
a) man who goes.
b) church and its leaders.
c) church and the Lord.

BELIEVERS SUPPORT WORKERS

Objective 4. *List the kinds of support which should be given to those sent out by the church.*

Workers sent by the church should be supported by the church. It would be sad if workers were sent out and then forgotten. The church must pray for its workers. Paul wrote to the church at Rome, "Join me in praying fervently to God for me" (Romans 15:30). To the church at Colossae, he wrote, "Pray also for us, so that God will give us a good opportunity to preach his

What the Church Does for the World

message" (Colossians 4:3). Workers who have been sent out are still part of the assembly. We must pray for them.

Paul also thanked the churches for sending him money. (See Romans 15:24, Philippians 2:25 and 4:15.) Workers who are sent out sometimes need money to do the work God has called them to do.

For You to Do

7 Circle the letter in front of the correct answers. When the workers were sent out by the early church, the church
a) supported them by gifts.
b) continued to pray for them.
c) criticized the results of their ministry.

8 a Write the name of a worker who was sent out by your church.

....

b Have you supported him with prayer and money? ....

The Church

9 Do you know of a tribe or area where the gospel of Christ is not known? Write its name here.

....

Jesus said, "There is a large harvest, but few workers to gather it in. Pray to the owner of the harvest that he will send out workers to gather it in" (Luke 10:2).

10 Look back over this entire lesson and list at least three duties that Christians have to unbelievers.

....

....

....

Check Your Answers

10 Any three of these:
Do good, thereby oppose evil.
Pray for the unbelievers.
Tell the good news.
Send workers.
Support workers.

1 a doing good deeds.
 b salt and light.
 c sin.
 d pray.

9 Your own answer.

2 a Tell the gospel.
 b Announce the good news.
 c An unhealthy church.

8 Your own answer.

3 Your own list of names.

7 a) supported them by gifts.
 b) continued to pray for them.

4 a Do good and therefore restrain evil.
 b Announce the good news.

6 c) church and the Lord.

5 c) go to those who have not heard the good news, whether nearby or far away.

lesson 8: what the church does for God

In Lesson 6, we studied how Christians help each other in the body of Christ. In Lesson 7, we saw some of our responsibilities to unbelievers. The church must do service for itself and others. Also, it must do special service for God.

In Lesson 1, we learned that one of God's purposes for the church is to bring glory to Himself. How can the church glorify its Lord? What does the church do to obey the Lord? These are some of the things we will look at in this lesson.

Christians who know how to pray should put their knowledge into action. Prayer is a service to God as well as a privilege for us. You know that you should worship and you like to worship, but sometimes you get too busy with other things.

If you are a Christian, you know the joy of obedience to Christ, and you feel guilty when you do not obey. Being obedient honors God. Let us honor Him!

In this lesson you will study...

Special Acts of Worship
The Believer's Baptism
The Lord's Supper

This lesson will help you...

- Define and illustrate worship.
- Describe the importance of baptism.
- Understand the meaning of the Lord's Supper.

SPECIAL ACTS OF WORSHIP

Objective 1. *Describe several ways we can worship God.*

In our first lesson, we learned that one of the purposes of the church is to praise God. Christians bring glory to God by their godly lives. As Paul said to the church at Philippi, "Your lives will be filled with the truly good qualities which only Jesus Christ can produce, for the glory and praise of God" (Philippians 1:11).

But Christians also glorify God by their worship. To worship means to pay respect, to honor, and to obey. We worship by praising God for His goodness. As Paul wrote to the church at Ephesus, "Let us praise God ... for the free gift he gave us in his dear Son!" (Ephesians 1:6). (See also Ephesians 1:12, 14.)

The Bible says that all believers are to be like priests offering prayer and praise to God. "You will serve as holy priests to offer spiritual and acceptable sacrifices to God through Jesus Christ" (1 Peter 2:5). The sacrifice which the church gives is praise. "Let us, then, always offer praise to God as our sacrifice through Jesus, which is the offering presented by lips that confess him as Lord" (Hebrews 13:15).

We also worship God by singing. The Bible says much about worshiping God in song. The whole book of Psalms is songs. One says "Sing to the Lord and praise him!" (Psalm 96:2). Paul may have had this

What the Church Does for God

passage in mind when he wrote to the church at Colossae, "Sing to God with thanksgiving in your hearts" (Colossians 3:16).

The Bible tells us about another way to worship God: by giving. Yes, giving is an act of worship. In his letter to the church at Philippi, Paul thanks them for their gift. He said, "Epaphroditus has brought me all your gifts. They are like a sweet-smelling offering to God, a sacrifice which is acceptable and pleasing to him" (Philippians 4:18). Because Christians give, needs are met. Because needs are met, people praise God. "For this service [of giving] you perform not only meets the needs of God's people, but also produces an outpouring of grateful thanks to God" (2 Corinthians 9:12).

For You to Do

Circle the letter in front of the correct answer.

1 To worship means to
   a) give money to worthy causes.
   b) attend church regularly.
   c) pay great honor to.
   d) be kind to people.

2 The basic purpose of the church is to
  a) bring glory to God.
  b) help people lead good lives.
  c) gather people for prayer.
  d) sing about God.

3 Which of the following is NOT a way to worship God?
  a) Singing God's praise
  b) Praising God's goodness
  c) Giving gifts for God's work
  d) Living an ungodly life

4 Complete the following sentence. Christians are to offer the sacrifice of ....

....

5 Make a list of some ways to praise God.

....

....

We must be careful here. True worship is not simply singing, praying, or giving. These are the outward signs of our worship. True worship is spiritual. We could go to a Christian meeting and sing, but never really worship. Jesus said, "God is Spirit, and only by the power of his Spirit can people worship him as he really is" (John 4:24). Worship is not form or ritual. Worship is spiritual. "We worship God by means of his Spirit and rejoice in our life in union with Christ Jesus. We do not put any trust in external ceremonies" (Philippians 3:3). Let us never confuse the activities associated with worship with its spiritual reality.

For You to Do

6 Choose the best answer of each two given in parentheses and write it in the blank.

a True worship is ....
(spiritual) (ceremonial)

b Christians worship by means of

....
(the Holy Spirit) (forms and rituals)

THE BELIEVER'S BAPTISM

Objective 2. *Explain why Christians should be baptized.*

When we express love to God, we are doing something to please Him. Our love and praise are better than ceremonies. However, Jesus did tell us to observe two ceremonies. These two ceremonies that Christ ordered are called ordinances. The one we will now consider is called *baptism*.

When a person becomes a Christian, he wants to tell everyone what he has done. Baptism is a way of doing this. Usually the pastor arranges a place for the baptism, such as a lake or stream. The new Christian is lowered into the water and brought up again. This is a picture of what Christ has done for the believer. The Christian is, by means of baptism, identified with

Christ's death and resurrection. Paul explained this to the church at Colossae:

> For when you were baptized, you were buried with Christ, and in baptism you were also raised with Christ through your faith in the active power of God, who raised him from death (Colossians 2:12).

So baptism is a sign to others that our old, sinful life is buried, and we now have a new life in Christ Jesus.

Baptism is *not* something done to unbelievers to make them believers. Baptism does not save a person from sin. It is not like magic.

In the early church, people believed in Christ, and then they were baptized. When the Holy Spirit first came upon the church, Peter preached the importance of faith in Christ. And "many of them believed his message and were baptized." Later Philip brought the message of Christ to Samaria. The Bible says, "When they believed Philip's message about the good news of the Kingdom of God and about Jesus Christ, they were baptized, both men and women" (Acts 8:12).

What the Church Does for God

Jesus commanded us to baptize new believers. "Go, then, to all peoples everywhere and make them my disciples: baptize them in the name of the Father, the Son, and the Holy Spirit" (Matthew 28:19). It is our duty to obey Him.

For You to Do

7 Read Romans 6:4 and fill in the following blanks:

By our baptism, then, we were .... with him and shared his .... in order that, just as Christ was .... by the glorious power of the Father, so also we might ....

8 Choose the best answer of each two given in parentheses and write it in the blank.
a The church baptizes because

....
(it is a ceremony) (Christ commanded it)

b Who should be baptized?

....
(Believers) (Unbelievers)

c Baptism ....
(makes people Christians) (shows what Christ did)

THE LORD'S SUPPER

Objective 3. *Explain the biblical meaning of the Lord's Supper.*

Jesus commanded the church to baptize. But Jesus also commanded us to observe the Lord's Supper. At this last meal with His disciples, He said "Do this in memory of me" (1 Corinthians 11:24).

Like baptism, the Lord's Supper is an ordinance. It is not magic. It is not an empty ceremony. When we observe the Lord's Supper we honor Christ.

When we share the bread and the cup, we show what Christ has done for us. Paul said that by it "you proclaim the Lord's death" (1 Corinthians 11:26). By this meal we show ourselves to be one with Christ. It helps us remember that Christ died for us.

> Then he took a piece of bread, gave thanks to God, broke it, and gave it to them saying, "This is my body, which is given for you. Do this in memory of me." In the same way, he gave them the cup after the supper, saying, "This cup is God's new

covenant sealed with my blood which is poured out for you" (Luke 22:19-20).

A person should not accept the bread and the cup until he has accepted Christ.

In this action, we are not only identified with Christ but with each other. The Lord's Supper is not something a person does alone. It shows the unity of the "body of Christ." Paul said:

When we drink from it (the cup), we are sharing in the blood of Christ. And the bread we break: when we eat it, we are sharing in the body of Christ. Because there is one loaf of bread, all of us, though many, are one body, for we all share the same loaf (1 Corinthians 10:16-17).

The Lord's Supper shows our faith in Christ's death, and in the unity of the church. But also, it shows our faith in Jesus' coming for His church. "You proclaim the Lord's death until he comes" (1 Corinthians 11:26).

For You to Do

9 Which of the following is NOT part of the meaning of the Lord's Supper?
   a) A picture of what Christ did for us
   b) An expression of faith in Christ's coming
   c) A way of getting forgiveness from God
   d) An expression of the unity of believers

10 The most important reason Christians observe the Lord's Supper and baptism is because
   a) they bring blessings to the Christian.
   b) they are religious ceremonies.
   c) they were commanded by Christ.
   d) they represent the Lord's death.

The church has a ministry to the Lord. It must obey and glorify the Lord. This work will not be finished until Jesus comes for His church. Then we will be with Him. Until that day, the church is needed to show believers and unbelievers what is the will of God. The church witnesses to the lost and strengthens the believers.

The early church did all these things. My heart is moved each time I read Acts 2:46-47

> Day after day they met as a group... they had their meals together in their homes, eating with glad and humble hearts, praising God, and enjoying the good will of all the people. And every day the Lord added to their group those who were being saved.

Can that be said about the church in my area? Or the church in your area? God wants to use us to help the church. He wants us to do our part.

Every Christian needs the church. "Let us not give up the habit of meeting together, as some are doing. Instead, let us encourage one another all the more" (Hebrews 10:25). The church is important to Christ. "Christ loved the church and gave his life for it" (Ephesians 5:25). Let us do our part in *His* church.

What the Church Does for God

Aren't you glad to be a part of His church? Now that we have come to the end of our study, I hope you have a better understanding of the church; its importance in bringing others to Christ; its value for you; its part in God's plan. Why don't you take time now to thank God for His church, the body of Christ. Let Him show you ways you can be more involved, and be a part of *His* plan for the church.

Check Your Answers

10 c) they were commanded by Christ.
 1 c) pay respect.
 9 c) A way of getting forgiveness from God.
 2 a) bring glory to God.

8 a Christ commanded it.
  b Believers.
  c shows what Christ did.

3 d) Living an ungodly life.

7 buried,
 death,
 raised from death,
 live a new life.

4 praise, worship.

6 a spiritual.
  b the Holy Spirit.

5 Living a godly life.
 Praising.
 Praying.
 Singing.
 Giving.

Now you are ready to fill out the last half of your student report for Lessons 5-8. Review these lessons, then follow the instructions in your student report. When you send your answer sheets to your instructor, ask him about another course of study.

CONGRATULATIONS!

You have finished this course. We hope that it has been a great help to you! Remember to complete the second section of your student report and return the answer sheet to your instructor. As soon as we receive both answer sheets we will check them over and send you your seal or certificate.

One Final Word

This is a special kind of book because it was written by people who care about you. These are happy people who have found good answers to many of the questions and problems which trouble almost everyone in the world. These happy people believe that God wants them to share with others the answers they have found. They believe that you need some important information in order to answer your own questions and problems and find the way of life that is best for you.

They have prepared this book in order to give you this information. You will find this book based on these fundamental truths:

1. You need a Savior. Read Romans 3:23, Exekiel 18:20.
2. You cannot save yourself. Read 1 Timothy 2:5, John 14:6.
3. God desires that the world should be saved. Read John 3:16-17.
4. God sent Jesus who gave his life to save all those who believe in Him. Read Galatians 4:4-5, 1 Peter 3:18.
5. The Bible shows us the way of salvation and teaches how to grow in the Christian life. Read John 15:5, John 10:10, 2 Peter 3:18.
6. You decide your eternal destiny. Read Luke 13:1-5, Matthew 10:32-33, John 3:35-36.

This book tells you how to decide your destiny, and it gives you opportunities to express your decision. Also, the book is different from others because it gives you a chance to contact people who prepared it. If you want to ask questions, or explain your needs and feelings, you may write to them.

In the back of the book you should find a card called *Decision Report and Request Card*. When you have made a decision, fill out the card and mail it as indicated. Then you will receive more help. You may use the card to ask questions, or make requests for prayer or information.

If there is no card in this copy of the book, write to your ICI instructor and you will receive a personal answer.

------Clip and send to your ICI instructor------

CL4140 The Church
Decision Report and Request Card

After studying this course, I have placed my trust in Jesus Christ as my Savior and Lord. I am returning this card with my signature and address to your ICI office for two reasons. First, to testify to my commitment to Christ and, second, to request information about more material to help me in my spiritual life.

NAME ....

ADDRESS ....

....

SIGNATURE ....

THE GREATEST OF ALL IS THE SERVANT OF ALL

Serving is an expression of love given to God for His consistent love. ICI courses are a vehicle of the Lord's that will assist you in developing into an effective and pleasing servant.

Using our courses will create an orderly system of Bible study and encourage a better understanding of spiritual truths.

To begin preparing for God's service we suggest enrolling in courses offered from our **Christian Service Program.**

Some courses from the **Christian Service Program** are:

CHRISTIAN MATURITY
THE KINGDOM, THE POWER AND THE GLORY
CORNERSTONES OF TRUTH
THE CHRISTIAN CHURCH IN MINISTRY
SPIRITUAL GIFTS
SOLVING LIFE'S PROBLEMS

If you desire a more detailed description about each course or directions on how to enroll in any of these courses contact your local ICI director.